Murphy's Law 2000

What else can go wrong in the 21th century!

Arthur Bloch

Illustrated by Tamara Petrosino

PSS!
PRICE STERN SLOAN
A member of Penguin Putnam Inc. New York

To my dear wife, Barbara.

Published by Price Stern Sloan, Inc.
a member of Penguin Putnam Inc.
375 Hudson Street
New York, NY 10014

Library of Congress Cataloging-in-Publication Data
Bloch, Arthur, date.
Murphy's law 2000: what else can go wrong in the 21th century! / Arthur Bloch.
p.   cm.
ISBN: 0-8431-7482-X
1. Murphy's law—Humor.   2. American wit and humor.
I. Title.   II. Title: Murphy's law two thousand.
PN6231.M82B565 1999   98-48575 CIP
818'.5402—dc21
Printed in the United States of America.
1 3 5 7 9 10 8 6 4 2

This book is printed on acid-free paper.

CONTENTS

FOREWORD

When I began compiling the Murphy's Law books in 1975, nobody had a personal computer, digital meant "of or pertaining to your fingers," and the Internet was just a malicious gleam in some teenager's eye. In those days, publishing was a technical field requiring intimate knowledge of design principles and pre-publication processes. Now you can create anything from a pamphlet that looks like a ransom note to a full-length novel without leaving home.

As Ogden Nash said, "Progress may have been all right once, but it went on too long." We should have quit before voice mail, Olestra® and spamming. (Meanwhile, things that could benefit from improvement, such as airline food or my golf swing, never change.)

In spite of our progress, it is seeming likely that we will reach the early stages at least of the next millennium—only the second time this has happened and the first time we've been able to express ourselves in print.

We've decided to publish this book several months before Y2K actually occurs. This way, in the unlikely event that all of our digital information turns to mush on January 1, we'll still have a paper record to remind us that things began to go wrong long before the information age. After all, what good is timeless wisdom if it's out of date the next year?

A note about the Laws: The main principle at work here (Bloch's Law of Eponymy) is, "the more insightful the observation, the greater the number of claimants to authorship." We've tried to be as accurate as possible in crediting the Laws, but we're not claiming to be definitive. We think you'll find the current volume has something for everybody, with a somewhat higher wisdom-to-wit ratio than in the past. We hope you enjoy it.

Arthur Bloch
Oakland, 1999

Murphology

MURPHY'S LAW:
If anything can go wrong, it will.

SCHNATTERLY'S SUMMING UP OF THE COROLLARIES:
If anything can't go wrong, it will.

PATRY'S LAW:
If you know something can go wrong, and take due precautions against it, something else will go wrong.

ROYSTER'S REFINEMENT OF MURPHY'S LAW:
When things go wrong somewhere, they are apt to go wrong everywhere.

NBC'S ADDENDUM TO MURPHY'S LAW:
You never run out of things that can go wrong.

LEAHY'S LAW:
If a thing is done wrong often enough, it becomes right.

ROTHMAN'S RULE:
When things go wrong, don't go with them.

LANNING'S LAW:
Murphy's Law always hits at the worst time

MURPHY'S TIME/ACTION QUANDARY:
You never know how soon it is too late.

MRS. MURPHY'S LAW:
If anything can go wrong, it will—when Mr. Murphy is away.

HAMPTON'S HOMILY:
The trouble with doing something right the first time is that nobody appreciates how difficult it was.

RUBENSTEIN'S LAW OF PUNCTUALITY:
Being punctual means only that your mistake will be made on time.

TUDISCO'S ASYMMETRY PRINCIPLE:
Things go wrong all at once, but things go right gradually.
Corollary: It takes no time at all to break something, but it takes forever to have something repaired.

JUAREZ'S LAWS:
1. Humans are the only animals able to retrace their steps to make the mistakes they had previously avoided.
2. The greater the number of people involved in an event, the less intelligent each of the participants becomes.

IRENE'S LAW:
There is no right way to do the wrong thing.

MCNULTY'S RULE:
First things first, but not necessarily in that order.

FORD'S ADVICE:
Failure is the opportunity to begin again more intelligently.

ZAHAS'S LAW OF TOPOLOGY:

The shortest distance between two points is a downward spiral.

FRESCO'S DISCOVERY:

If you knew what you were doing, you'd probably be bored.

Corollary: Just because you're bored doesn't mean you know what you're doing.

LEE'S LAW:

It takes less time to do something right than it takes to explain why you did it wrong.

LAW OF CONSERVATION OF TSOURIS:

The amount of aggravation in the universe is a constant.

Corollary: If things are going well in one area, they are going wrong in another.

STEWART'S COROLLARIES:

1. Murphy's Law may be delayed or suspended for an indefinite period of time, provided that such delay or suspension will result in a greater catastrophe at a later date.

2. The magnitude of the catastrophe is directly proportional to the number of people watching.

3. The magnitude of the catastrophe is exponentially proportional to the importance of the occasion.

4. If an outcome has a 50% chance of occurring, its actual probability of happening is inversely proportional to the desirability of the outcome.

5. If two corollaries of Murphy's Law contradict each other, the one with greater potential for damage takes precedence.

CAMPBELL'S LAW:
   The less you do, the less can go wrong.

LONG'S LAW:
   Natural laws have no pity.

BALDRIDGE'S LAW:
   If we knew what we were getting into we would never get into anything.

COOKE'S LAW:
   It is always hard to notice what isn't there.

PHILO'S LAW:
   To learn from your mistakes, you must first realize that you are making mistakes.

MURRAY'S LAW:
   If at first you don't succeed, skydiving is not for you.

WOLF'S LAW OF PLANNING:
   A good place to start from is where you are.

HOFSTADTER'S LAW:
   Things always take longer than you anticipate, even if you take into account Hofstadter's Law.

DUNN'S LAW:
   Careful planning is no substitute for dumb luck.

GILBERTSON'S LAW:
   Nothing is foolproof to a sufficiently talented fool.

BARBER'S RULE:
   Anything worth doing is worth doing to excess.

MELNICK'S LAW:
If at first you do succeed, try not to look too astonished.

FINAGLE'S LAW ACCORDING TO NIVEN:
The perversity of the universe tends to a maximum.

THE LAW OF EPONYMY:
Any given Law will not be named for the person who created it.

Corollary: It's not who said it, it's who named it.

KEYES'S FIRST AXIOM:
Any quotation that can be changed will be.

GeNeraL ProbLeMatics

KELLEY'S LAW:
Nothing is ever as simple as it first seems.

JONES'S LAW:
Experience enables you to recognize a mistake when you make it again.

CANNON'S CANON:
Experience is what causes you to make new mistakes instead of old ones.

BERYL'S SECOND LAW:
It's always easy to see both sides of an issue we are not particularly concerned about.

MCGUFFIN'S LAW:
It's easy to see the bright side of other people's problems.

APPLE'S LAW OF RECOVERY:
You can't recover from a problem you don't have.

SEVENTH LAW OF PRODUCT DESIGN:
No problem is so large that it can't be fit in somewhere.

HERMAN'S LAW:
A good scapegoat is almost as good as a solution.

EINSTEIN ON PROBLEMATICS:
    We can't solve problems by using the same kind of thinking we used when we created them.

BACON'S MAXIM:
    Truth comes out of error more easily than out of confusion.

BOHR'S AXIOM:
    The opposite of a profound truth may well be another profound truth.

THE FIRST RULE OF EXCAVATION:
    If you are in a hole, stop digging.

MANLY'S MAXIM:
Logic is a systematic method of coming to the wrong conclusion with confidence.

GARDENER'S PHILOSOPHY:
Brilliant opportunities are cleverly disguised as insolvable problems.
Corollary: The reverse is also true.

ISSAWI-WILCOX PRINCIPLE:
Problems increase in geometric ratio, solutions in arithmetic ratio.

GOLD'S LAW OF JOURNALISM:
A column about errors will contain errors.

BIG AL'S LAW:
A good solution can be successfully applied to almost any problem.

PRIMARY POLITICAL COROLLARY:
A good slogan beats a good solution.

ELDRIDGE'S LAW OF WAR:
Man is always ready to die for an idea, provided that the idea is not quite clear to him.

BARRY'S RULE:
If you stop to think, remember to start again.

THE KIBBITZER'S RULE:
It is much easier to suggest solutions when you know nothing about the problem.

MARGOT'S LAW:
Advice is what we ask for when we already know the answer but wish we didn't.

DEITZ'S LAW OF EGO:

The fury engendered by the misspelling of a name in a column is in direct ratio to the obscurity of the mentionee.

MENCKEN'S MAXIM:

There's always an easy solution to every human problem—neat, plausible, and wrong.

EXpertSMaNSHip & AcadeMioLogy

WHITEHEAD'S RULE:
Seek simplicity, and distrust it.

MULLINS'S OBSERVATION:
Indecision is the key to flexibility.

THE MUNROE DOCTRINE:
A little inaccuracy sometimes saves tons of explanation.

BUECHNER'S PRINCIPLE:
The simplest explanation is that it just doesn't make sense.

BOHR'S LAW:
An expert is someone who has made all of the possible mistakes in a very narrow field of study.

RYAN'S LAW:
Make three correct guesses consecutively and you will establish yourself as an expert.

LAGUARDIA'S LAW:
Statistics are like expert witnesses—they will testify for either side.

PIRSIG'S POSTULATE:
Data without generalization is just gossip.

LAW OF RETROSPECTION:
You can never tell which way the train went by looking at the track.

UTVICH'S LAW:
One accurate measurement is worth a thousand expert opinions.

THE JONES/EINSTEIN PRINCIPLE:
Originality is the art of concealing your source.

NOBEL EFFECT:
There is no proposition, no matter how foolish, for which a dozen Nobel signatures cannot be collected.
Corollary: Any such petition is guaranteed page-one treatment in the *New York Times*.

FUDD'S FIRST LAW OF CREATIVITY:
To get a good idea, get lots of ideas.
Duff's Counter-Law: The more ideas you have, the more difficulty you will have recognizing the good ones.

ULMANN'S RAZOR:
When stupidity is a sufficient explanation, there is no need to have recourse to any other.

COUVIER'S LAW:
There is nothing more frightening than ignorance in action.

PHILLIPS'S RULE:
The best defense against logic is ignorance.

TUCKER'S COMMENT:
It makes sense, when you don't think about it.

WILDE ON ADVICE:
The only thing to do with good advice is pass it on. It is never any use to oneself.

VON NEUMANN'S AXIOM:
There's no sense in being precise when you don't know what you're talking about.

TATMAN'S RULE:
Always assume that your assumption is invalid.

YOUNG'S RULE OF ARGUMENT:
They can't agree with you if you don't agree with them.

DE BEAUMARCHAIS'S MOTTO:
It is not necessary to understand things in order to argue about them.

WEBER'S MAXIM:
A single fact can spoil a good argument.

THE WHISPERED RULE:
People will believe anything if you whisper it.

HOWE'S THEORY:
There is some advice that is too good—the advice to love your enemies, for example.

TWAIN ON FACTS:
Get your facts first, and then you can distort them as much as you please.

T. S. ELIOT'S OBSERVATION:
Some editors are failed writers, but so are most writers.

CAMUS'S LAW:

Those who write clearly have readers. Those who write obscurely have commentators.

PRESCHER'S LAW OF EXAMS:

If you don't know the answer, someone will ask the question.

THE STUDENT'S TAUTOLOGY:

The teacher is never absent on the day of the exam.

HERRNSTEIN'S LAW:

The attention paid to an instructor is a constant regardless of the size of the class; thus, as the class swells, the amount of attention paid per student drops in direct ratio.

DILLING'S LAW:

Whenever an erroneous word or letter can change the entire meaning of a sentence, the error will be in the direction of greatest embarassment.

DOLIN'S LAW OF RESEARCH:

The library will have every back issue of a magazine except for the issue you need for your research.

KISSINGER'S AXIOM:

University politics are vicious precisely because the stakes are so small.

COLEMAN'S COMMENTARY ON SANTAYANA:

Those who fail to learn from the past are condemned to repeat history class.

PLUTARCH'S RULE:
It is impossible for anyone to learn that which he thinks he already knows.

GROYA'S LAW:
What we learn after we know it all is what counts.

THE TWO RULES FOR ULTIMATE SUCCESS IN LIFE:
1. Never tell everything you know.

StateSMaNSHip

MARSHALL'S FIRST LAW OF THE LEGISLATURE:

Never let the facts get in the way of a carefully thought out bad decision.

FRANCE'S RULE OF FOLLY:

If a million people believe a foolish thing, it is still a foolish thing.

SANTAYANA'S OBSERVATION:

Fanaticism consists of redoubling your efforts when you have forgotten your aim.

CALVIN COOLIDGE'S COMMENT:

You don't have to explain something you never said.

ADLER'S RULE:

It is easier to fight for one's principles than to live up to them.

RUSSELL ON PATRIOTISM:

Patriotism is the willingness to kill and be killed for trivial reasons.

MAIN'S LAW:

For every action there is an equal and opposite government program.

ARMEY'S AXIOM:

You can't get ahead while getting even.

BOOKER T. WASHINGTON'S RULE:

You can't hold a man down without staying down with him.

L.B.J.'S LAW:

If two men agree on everything, you may be sure that only one of them is doing the thinking.

INGE'S AXIOM:

It is useless for sheep to pass resolutions in favor of vegetarianism while wolves remain of a different opinion.

HEINE'S LAW:
One should forgive one's enemies, but not before they are hanged.

AMERINGER'S AXIOM:
Politics is the gentle art of getting votes from the poor and campaign funds from the rich by promising to protect each from the other.

THOMAS JEFFERSON'S RULE:
Delay is preferable to error.

THE OIL SPILL PRINCIPLE:
People will accept any bad news if the magnitude of the disaster is revealed gradually.

LOVKA'S FIRST POLITICAL PRINCIPLE:
There is no sincerity like a politician telling a lie.

CAMERON'S LAW:
An honest politician is one who, when he is bought, will stay bought.

DUCK'S POLITICAL PRINCIPLE:
Any campaign reform only lasts until the powers regroup.

ABOUREZK'S LAWS OF POLITICS:
1. Don't worry about your enemies. It's your allies who will do you in.
2. The bigger the appropriations bill, the shorter the debate.
3. If you want to curry favor with a politician, give him credit for something that someone else did.

PEROT'S OBSERVATION:
The only thing most politicians stand for is re-election.

STORRY'S PRINCIPLE OF CRIMINAL BEHAVIOR:
The degree of guilt is directly proportional to the intensity of the denial.

NOWLAN'S LAW:
Following the path of least resistance is what makes politicians and rivers crooked.

SHAFFER'S LAW:
The effectiveness of a politician varies in inverse proportion to his commitment to principle.

HUNTER'S LAW:
No matter how dishonorable, every politician considers himself honorable.

WILSON'S LAW OF POLITICS:
If you want to make enemies, try to change something.

POLITICAL POLLSTER'S RULES:
1. When the polls are in your favor, flaunt them.
2. When the polls are overwhelmingly unfavorable, (a) ridicule and dismiss them; or (b) stress the volatility of public opinion.
3. When the polls are slightly unfavorable, play for sympathy as a struggling underdog.
4. When it's too close to call, be surprised at your own strength.

TUPPER'S POLITICAL POSTULATE:

Those who sit astride the fence have few directions from which to choose.

EVAN'S LAW:

Once you give up integrity, the rest is easy.

LAWRENCE'S LAW:

A diplomat is someone who can tell you to go to hell in such a way that you will look forward to the trip.

PODNOS'S LAW:

One is tolerant only of that which does not concern him.

SYRUS'S LEADERSHIP PRINCIPLE:

Anyone can hold the helm when the sea is calm.

POULOS'S POLITICAL COROLLARY:

A good slogan beats a good solution.

GALBRAITH'S LAW OF POLITICS:

Anyone who says he isn't going to resign four times, definitely will.

GALBRAITH'S LAW OF PROMINENCE:

Getting on the cover of *Time* guarantees the existence of opposition in the future.

LAW OF GOVERNMENTAL SELF-FULFILLMENT:

The more money spent on the feasibility study, the more feasible the project.

SHAW'S POLITICAL PRINCIPLE:

A government that robs Peter to pay Paul can always depend on the support of Paul.

NADER'S LAW:

The speed of exit of a civil servant is directly proportional to the quality of his service.

SANRIO'S FIRST RULE OF GOVERNMENT PROGRAMS:

A bureaucratic program that does not work stands the best chance of being expanded.

NOBLE'S LAW OF POLITICS:

All other things being equal, a bald man cannot be elected President of the United States.

Corollary: Given a choice between two bald political candidates, the American people will vote for the less bald of the two.

MIRAGLIA'S RULE OF LAW:

Never make a major policy change based on a close vote.

POTTER'S LAW:

A rumor doesn't gain credence until it's officially denied.

NAPOLEAN'S OBSERVATION:

Rascality has limits; stupidity has not.

ReSearcHMaNSHip

SY'S LAW OF SCIENCE:
Sometimes it takes several years to recognize the obvious.

BATES'S LAW OF RESEARCH:
Research is the process of going up alleys to see if they're blind.

VON BRAUN'S CREDO:
Research is what I'm doing when I don't know what I'm doing.

WESTHEIMER'S DISCOVERY:
A couple of months in the laboratory can frequently save a couple of hours in the library.

LAND'S LEMMA:
When the experiment doesn't work, distrust the experiment; when the experiment works, distrust the theory.

GELL-MANN'S DICTUM:
Whatever isn't forbidden is required.
Corollary: If there's no reason why something shouldn't exist, then it must exist.

ALAN'S LAW OF RESEARCH:
The theory is supported as long as the funds are.

BERSHADER'S LAW:
Experiment and theory often show remarkable agreement when performed in the same laboratory.

THOMPSON'S THEORY:
Any theory can be made to fit any fact by incorporating additional assumptions.

HORWOOD'S SIXTH LAW:
If you have the right data, you have the wrong problem.

FEYNEMAN'S LAW:
Science is the belief in the ignorance of the experts.

FIRST RULE OF APPLIED MATHEMATICS:
Ninety-eight percent of all statistics are made up.

GERROLD'S LAWS OF DYNAMICS:

1. An object in motion will be headed in the wrong direction.

2. An object at rest will be in the wrong place.

3. The energy required to change either of these states will be more than you wish to expend, but not so much as to make the task totally impossible.

PUGH'S LAW:

If the human brain were simple enough for us to understand it, we would be too simple to understand it.

THOMAS HUXLEY'S RULE OF PROGRESS:

Every great advance in natural knowledge has involved the absolute rejection of authority.

MCFEE'S MAXIM:

Matter can neither be created nor destroyed. However, it can be lost.

PROOF TECHNIQUES:
1. Proof by referral to nonexistent authorities.
2. Reduction ad nauseam.
3. Proof by assignment.
4. Method of least astonishment.
5. Proof by handwaving.
6. Proof by intimidation.
7. Method of deferral until later in the course.
8. Proof by reduction to a sequence of unrelated lemmas.
9. Method of convergent irrelevancies.

KEPLER'S LAW OF ECOLOGY:
Nature uses as little as possible of anything.

THE RATIONAL FALLACY:
Everything happens for a reason.

CHANEY'S LAW:
Entropy requires no maintenance.

EINSTEIN ON MATH AND SCIENCE:
1. The whole of science is nothing more than a refinement of everyday thinking.
2. Technological progress is like an axe in the hands of a pathological criminal.
3. If A is a success in life, then A equals x plus y plus z. Work is x; y is play; and z is keeping your mouth shut.
4. As far as the laws of mathematics refer to reality, they are not certain; as far as they are certain, they do not refer to reality.
5. Two things are infinite: the universe and human stupidity; and I'm not sure about the universe.

DYER'S LAW OF RELATIVITY:
Life is short, but a three-hour movie is interminable.

THORNLEY'S LAW:
What we imagine is order is merely the prevailing form of chaos.

VON BRAUN'S ADVICE:
I have learned to use the word "impossible" with the greatest caution.

FIRST RULE OF ENVIRONMENTAL PROTECTION:
The species is protected only after it is hopelessly depleted.

SECOND RULE OF ENVIRONMENTAL PROTECTION:

The most efficient way to dispose of toxic waste is to reclassify the waste as non-toxic.

THIRD RULE OF ENVIRONMENTAL PROTECTION (THE CATALYTIC CONVERTER PRINCIPLE):

Anything done to improve one area of the environment will cause corresponding damage in another area.

WALDER'S OBSERVATION:

A mathematician is one who is willing to assume everything except responsibility.

ALBINAK'S ALGORITHM:

When graphing a function, the width of the line should be inversely proportional to the precision of the data.

GRIFFIN'S LAW:

Statistics are a logical and precise method for saying a half-truth inaccurately.

Techno-Murphology & Designsmanship

BAKER'S RULE:
Inanimate objects are classified scientifically into three major categories: those that don't work, those that break down, and those that get lost.

O'ROURKE'S RULE:
Never fight an inanimate object.

RALPH'S OBSERVATION:
It is a mistake to allow any mechanical object to realize that you are in a hurry.

SHAND'S LAW:
The more efficiently a project is done, the greater the chance it will have to be undone.

LUCKY'S LAW OF MECHANICS:
After spending 45 minutes on a repair, you discover a 5-minute way to do it.

EDISON'S OBSERVATION:
Opportunity is missed by most people because it is dressed in overalls and looks like work.

LEE'S LAW OF ELECTRICAL REPAIR:
The simpler it looks, the more problems it hides.

ENDO'S BETAMAX PRINCIPLE:
If there are two competing and incompatible technologies on the market, the inferior technology will prevail.

GOURHAN'S LAW OF TECHNOLOGY:
The degree of technical competence is inversely proportional to the level of management.

MCAULEY'S AXIOM:
If a system is of sufficient complexity, it will be built before it is designed, implemented before it is tested, and outdated before it is debugged.

THE STAGES OF SYSTEMS DEVELOPMENT:
1. Wild enthusiasm.
2. Disillusionment.
3. Total confusion.
4. Search for the guilty.
5. Punishment of the innocent.
6. Promotion of the non-participants.

ARNOLD'S LAWS OF DOCUMENTATION:
1. If it should exist, it doesn't.
2. If it does exist, it's out of date.
3. Only useless documentation transcends the first two laws.

ACKERMAN'S LAW OF THE TOOLBOX:
The single odd-sized nut, bolt or screw which you have seen every time you open your toolbox will disappear on the day a job calls for that particular size.

RIVES'S RULE:
Everything falls apart on the same day.

RANDY'S RULE:

A ton of anything is ugly.

MORRIS'S ASSEMBLY PARADOX:

If you put it together correctly the first time, there was something you should have done before you put it together.

THE EXTRA-PART PRINCIPLE:

You never know what that extra part is for until you've thrown it away.

BOWERSOX'S LAW OF THE WORKSHOP:

If you have only one nail, it will bend.

SECOND LAW OF THE WORKSHOP:

You can always find three nuts to fit the four screws you need.

SAUL'S SAW:

When fastening down something held by several screws, don't tighten any of them until they are all in place.

COULL'S COMMENT:

Every new project requires a tool that you don't have.

THOREAU'S OBSERVATION:

Men have become the tools of their tools.

LAW OF PRODUCT TESTING:

A component selected at random from a group having 99% reliability will be a member of the 1% group.

KAGEL'S LAW:

Anything adjustable will eventually need adjustment.

THE MACHINE RULES:

1. Nothing will work that is put back together in the reverse of the way it was dismantled.

2. The last turn on any nut or bolt will strip it or snap it off.

Corollary: Without the last turn, the nut or bolt will fall off.

CAMPBELL'S MAXIM:

Hell is the place where everything tests perfectly and nothing works.

FIFTH LAW OF DESIGN:

Design flaws travel in groups.

SLOAN'S LAW:

The changes in new models should be so attractive as to create dissatisfaction with past models.

CoMpUter MurpHoLogy & LaWS oF tHe InterNet

CRAYNE'S LAW:
All computers wait at the same speed.

ROBBINS'S RULE:
One good reason why computers can do more work than people is that they never have to stop and answer the phone.

BELINDA'S LAW:
The chance of a computer crash is directly proportional to the importance of the document that you are working on.

PICKERING'S LAW OF DATA LOSS:
The probability of a hard disk crashing increases in direct proportion to the amount of time since the drive was last backed up.

BREZNIKAR'S LAW OF COMPUTER TECHNOLOGY:
Applying computer technology is simply finding the right wrench to pound in the correct screw.

HAGAN'S LAW:
The attention span of a computer is only as long as its electrical cord.

THE UPGRADE PRINCIPLE:

The upgrade will break down as soon as the old version is deleted.

Corollary: The old version will not reinstall.

MURPHY'S COMPUTER SYSTEM DEFINITIONS:

Hardware: The parts of a computer system that can be kicked.

Software: The parts of a computer system that don't work.

Hard Disk: The part of a computer system that freezes up at the worst possible time.

Peripherals: The parts that are incompatible with your computer system.

Printer: The part of the computer system that jams when you're not looking.

Cable: The part of the computer system that is too short.

Mouse: See *cursing*.

Backup: An operation that is never performed on time.

Restore: A procedure that works perfectly until it is needed.

Memory: The part of a computer system that is insufficient.

Error Message: A request to OK the destruction of your own data.

File: The part of the computer system that cannot be found.

Processor: The part of a computer system that is obsolete.

Manual: The element of your computer system that is incomprehensible.

THOMPSON'S STEADY STATE THEORY:

The steady state of disks is full.

THE VIRUS FACTOR:

The one file you don't scan for viruses will be the one with the worst virus.

CROMER'S LAW:
A digital readout provides misinformation with greater accuracy than previously possible.

FINAGLE'S LAWS OF INFORMATION:
1. The information you have is not what you want.
2. The information you want is not what you need.
3. The information you need is not what you can obtain.
4. The information you can obtain costs more than you want to pay.

J. T.'S LAW OF TECHNICAL SUPPORT:
The better the customer service, the sooner you get to speak with someone who can't help you.

THORSON'S LAW:

The greater the emergency, the lower the charge in your cell-phone battery.

THE PRINTING LAWS:

1. It will not work the first time.
2. It probably will not work on the second attempt.
3. Immediately after you walk away from the printer, the paper will jam.

BRADLEY'S BROMIDE:

If computers get too powerful, we can organize them into a committee—that will do them in.

LUCAS'S LAWS:

1. Your most important program will require more memory than you have.
2. If you have enough memory, you will not have enough disk space.
3. If a program actually fits in memory and has enough disk space, it will crash.
4. If the program is running perfectly, it is waiting for a critical moment before it crashes.

MAZUR'S LAW:

No matter how low the price of the computer you purchased, you will find a more powerful computer for a lower price within one week of your purchase.

MOORE'S LAW (SIMPLIFIED):

Computer power doubles and prices halve every eighteen months.

PERLIS'S POSTULATE:

The computing field is always in need of new cliches.

PERKINS'S POSTULATE:

On-line tech support is designed to provide everything short of actual help.

THE PROGRAMMER'S DILEMMA:

Programming is like sex: One mistake and you're providing support for a lifetime.

EIGHTH LAW OF PROGRAMMING:

It is easier to change the specification to fit the program than vice versa.

PRINCIPLE OF OPERATING SYSTEMS:

Computers are an intelligence sink; there is no level of genius that cannot find its match in system design.
The Microsoft Corollary: It takes hundreds of geniuses to make a complex thing simple.

FLON'S LAW:

There is no language in which it is the least bit difficult to write bad programs.

KNOWLES'S LAWS:

1. The number of bogus selections returned on a search increases exponentially with the urgency of your search.
2. The number of bogus meta tag descriptors and keywords doubles monthly so that no searches will be meaningful after the year 2000.
3. Proper use of language, especially spelling and grammar, declines as technology advances.

LIZ'S LAW:

If you spend hours trying to sign on to a busy server, your connection will be lost as soon as you get on.

METCALFE'S LAW:

The value of a Net goes up as the square of the number of people on that Net.

SCHYER'S LAW OF RELATIVITY FOR PROGRAMMERS:

If the code and the comments disagree, then both are probably wrong.

ERICKSON'S EQUIVALENT:

Surfing the Internet is like spending an entire day at a magazine rack.

BALCH'S LAW:

Your new hardware won't run your old software.

HOLTEN'S DOWNLOAD PRINCIPLE:

The likelihood of receiving an error message during a download increases the closer you come to finishing.

THE DOWNLOAD FACTOR:

If a file takes an hour to download, someone in your house will pick up the phone in the 59th minute.

HITCH'S INTERNET LAW:

When connecting to a website, your request will take the most indirect possible route.

PETZEN'S INTERNET LAW:

The most promising result from a search engine query will lead to a dead link.

PICASSO'S POSTULATE:

Computers are useless. All they give you is answers.

THROOP'S AXIOM:

The universe is not user-friendly.

REASNER'S LAW OF THE INTERNET:

The probability of your browser locking up is directly proportional to how close you are to the information that you've been searching for.

HOROWITZ'S RULE:

A computer makes as many mistakes in two seconds as twenty men working twenty years.

THE 401 ERROR PRINCIPLE:

Your favorite bookmarks no longer exist on the server.

MCMAHON'S RULE:

No matter what you search for, at least one porn site will match your criteria.

RECTOR'S LAW OF E-MAIL:
Typos are not noticed until after the "Send" button has been hit.

SCHAAF'S LAW OF ONLINE RESEARCH:
Any quote found twice on the Internet will have two different wordings, attributions, or both.
Corollary: If the wording and source are consistent in two places, they are both wrong.

SULLIVAN'S LEMMA:
Artificial intelligence is no match for natural stupidity.

Socio-Murphology

LA ROCHEFOUCAULD'S RULE:
We all have the strength to endure the misfortune of others.

MORRIS'S LAW:
Anyone can admit to themselves they were wrong—the true test is admitting it to someone else.

JEROME'S RULE:
It is always the best policy to speak the truth—unless of course you are an exceptionally good liar.

MICKELS'S LAW:
Man invented language to satisfy his need to complain.

AGRAIT'S LAW:
A rumor will travel fastest to the place where it will do the most damage.

MIZNER'S LAW:
Misery loves company, but company does not reciprocate.

THE GUEST RULE:
Never mistake endurance for hospitality.

AUSTIN'S LAW:
Anything tastes better in someone else's house.

PHINNEY'S LAW:

The announcement for the one event you most wanted to attend will arrive in the mail the day after the event.

BEIRCE'S DEFINITION:

A boor is a person who talks when you wish him to listen.

A TWAIN OBSERVATION:

Good breeding consists of concealing how much we think of ourselves and how little we think of the other person.

LAW OF ASPERSION:

If you say something bad about someone, you will discover that the same criticism applies to you.

Corollary: The only faults that bother us in others are faults we share.

BROWN'S RULE:

Never offend people with style when you can offend them with substance.

ARLEN'S LAW:

It's amazing how nice people are to you when they know you're going away.

GOLDSTICK'S RULE:

Be kind to everyone you talk with. You never know who's going to be on the jury.

CROMER'S LAW:

People who don't believe in anything will believe the worst of other people.

HUBBARD'S HOMILY:

A friend is someone who knows all about you and still likes you.

LOGAN'S LAMENT:

Even the best of friends cannot attend each other's funeral.

MAUGHAM'S OBSERVATION:

It is easier to give up good habits than bad ones.

MURPHY'S FIRST LAW OF DIETING:

The first pounds you lose are in areas in which you didn't want to lose them.

MCDOUGAL'S RULE:

To be popular, give people good news about their bad habits.

LOVKA'S OTHER ADVICE:

Never rely on a person who uses "party" as a verb.

LIZ TAYLOR'S OBSERVATION:

The problem with people who have no vices is that generally you can be pretty sure they're going to have some pretty annoying virtues.

ONASSIS'S AXIOM:

If women didn't exist, all the money in the world would have no meaning.

NORMAN'S LAW:

No man knows what true happiness is until he gets married. By then, of course, it's too late.

TRISTAN'S LAW:
Appealingness is inversely proportional to attainability.

THE PURITAN PRINCIPLE:
If it feels good, don't do it.

YASENEK'S OBSERVATION:
Kissing is a means of getting two people so close together that they can't see anything wrong with each other.

SANTAYANA'S SECOND LAW:
When men and women agree, it is only in their conclusions. Their reasons are always different.

JANDA'S LAW:
When you finally meet the perfect woman, she will be waiting for the perfect man.

THE FEMINIST DICTUM:
A woman without a man is like a fish without a bicycle.

FRIEDMAN'S RESPONSE TO THE FEMINIST DICTUM:
A man without a woman is like a neck without a pain.

THE FERTILITY FACTOR:
Women are only fertile a few days each month—unless they're single.

RITA MAE BROWN'S OBSERVATION:
If this were a logical world, men would ride sidesaddle.

SARAH'S LAW:
You never begin your summer romance until the last day of summer.

BUreaucratics, Hierarchiology & Committology

YOUNG'S RULE OF DELEGATION:
When moving a pregnant cat, pick up the cat and let her take care of the kittens.

PLANER'S RULE:
An exception granted becomes a right expected the next time it is requested.

ACHESON'S RULE OF THE BUREAUCRACY:
A memorandum is written not to inform the reader but to protect the writer.

ROBERT'S RULE OF CORPORATE MANAGEMENT:
Title outweighs performance.

WILSON'S LAW:
A person's rank is in inverse relation to the speed of his speech.

MOSELEY'S LAW:
Executive behavior is based on the managerial myth that future organizational expansion will resolve past institutional incompetence.

FIFTH RULE OF SUCCESS IN BUSINESS:
Keep your boss's boss off your boss's back.

THIRD LAW OF PRODUCTIVITY:

When the bosses talk about improving productivity, they are never talking about themselves.

ROBERTSON'S RULE OF BUREACRACY:
The more directives you issue to solve a problem, the worse it gets.

GRIZZARD'S SLED-DOG PRINCIPLE:
Only the lead dog gets a change of scenery.

PRINCE'S PRINCIPLE:
People who work sitting down are paid more than people who work standing up.

STEINER'S POSTULATES:
1. In business, as well as in chess, the winner is the one who makes the next to last mistake.
2. At business meetings, the one unmatched asset is the ability to yawn with your mouth closed.
3. Consistency is the last refuge of the unimaginative.
4. Trivial matters take up more time because we know more about them than important matters.

WELLER'S RULE FOR BUREAUCRATIC FUNDING:

Never admit that your activity has sufficient staff, space, or budget.

ENGLE'S LAW:

When you stand up to be counted, someone will take your seat.

ANDERSON'S LAWS OF SURVIVAL FOR LOW-LEVEL MANAGERS:

1. Never be too right too often.
2. Hints are better taken than given.

SECOND LAW OF THE CORPORATION:

Any action for which there is no logical explanation will be deemed "company policy."

CHAPMAN'S LAW:

Don't be irreplaceable. If you can't be replaced, you can't be promoted.

OWENS'S LAW:

If you are good, you will be assigned all the work. If you are really good, you will get out of it.

LEVIN'S LAW:

Following the rules will not get the job done.
Corollary: Getting the job done is no excuse for not following the rules.

MCCARTHY'S MAXIM:

The only thing that saves us from the bureaucracy is its inefficiency.

THE CHIEF EXECUTIVE IN CHARGE OF TITLES LAW:

The longer the title, the less important the job.

LAW OF CORPORATE TAKEOVERS:

In any corporate buyout, the resultant company will provide inferior service and quality.

Corollaries:

1. The larger the company that takes over, the less attention is paid to projects ongoing before the takeover.

2. When they say no jobs will be lost, they are lying.

VAN ROY'S LAW:

A meeting is no substitute for progress.

ROBERT'S RULE:

An efficient bureaucracy is the greatest threat to liberty.

ADLER'S AXIOM:

Language is all that separates us from the lower animals—and from the bureaucrats.

SANRIO'S RULE OF BUREAUCRATIC FUNDING (AKA THE SERVE THYSELF SOLUTION):

The first expenditure of new revenue made available to a bureaucratic agency will be used to expand the administration of the program rather than the needs of the program itself.

GAMMON'S LAW:

In a bureaucratic system, increase in expenditure will be matched by fall in production.

NIES'S LAW:

The effort expended by a bureaucracy in defending any error is in direct proportion to the size of the error.

HERBERT'S LAW:

A bureaucracy is an organization that has raised stupidity to the status of a religion.

COBLITZ'S LAW:

A committee can make a decision that is dumber than any of its members.

BROWNIAN MOTION RULE OF BUREAUCRACIES:

It is impossible to distinguish, from a distance, whether the bureaucrats associated with your project are simply sitting on their hands, or frantically trying to cover their asses.

Heisenberg's Addendum: If you observe a bureaucrat closely enough to make the distinction above, he will react to your observation by covering his ass.

PHILLIP'S LAW OF COMMITTEE PROCEDURE:

The only changes that are easily adopted are changes for the worse.

COCKS'S COMMENT:

A committee is a cul-de-sac down which ideas are lured and then quietly strangled.

MAYNARD'S FIRST RULE OF COMMITTEES:

The effectiveness of a committee is in inverse proportion to the number of its members.

BODRUG'S LAW:

No one has ever erected a monument to a committee.

TRAHEY'S LAW:

Never dump a good idea on a conference table. It will belong to the conference.

PETERSON'S PRINCIPLE:

Never delay the ending of a meeting or the beginning of a dinner hour.

HORWOOD'S NINTH LAW:

Acquisition of knowledge from experience is an exception.

HORWOOD'S EIGHTH LAW:

In complex systems, there is no relationship between information gathered and decisions made.

CHAPMAN'S COMMITTEE RULES:

1. Never arrive on time, or you will be stamped a beginner.
2. Don't say anything until the meeting is half over; this stamps you as being wise.
3. Be as vague as possible; this prevents irritating others.
4. When in doubt, suggest that a subcommittee be appointed.
5. Be the first to move for adjournment; this will make you popular—it's what everyone is waiting for.

WOLINSKI'S LAW:

Teamwork is wasting half of one's time explaining to others why they are wrong.

Office Murphology

SLOUS'S LAW:
If you do a job too well, you will get stuck with it.

FRANKO'S LAW OF THE WORKPLACE:
If you enjoy what you're doing, you're probably doing it wrong.

LARSON'S BUREAUCRATIC PRINCIPLE:
Accomplishing the impossible means only that the boss will add it to your regular duties.

THE FIRST PITFALL OF GENIUS:
No boss will keep an employee who is right all the time.

PERKIN'S LAW:
A pat on the back is only a few centimeters from a kick in the butt.

RAPHEL'S LAW OF BUSINESS:
The less the staff has to do, the slower they do it.

CHANDLER'S LAW:
The more crap you put up with, the more crap you are going to get.

GRANDE'S LAW:
Always do exactly what your boss would do if he knew what he was talking about.

MOSELY'S LAW:

Accidents happen when two people try to be clever at the same time.

ROBINSON'S LAW:

The guy you beat out of a prime parking spot is the one you have to see for the job interview.

LAMPNER'S LAW OF EMPLOYMENT:

When leaving work late, you will go unnoticed. When leaving work early, you will meet your boss in the parking lot.

THE OFFICE MAXIM:

The phone never rings when you have nothing to do.

THE IRON LAW OF SECRETARIES:

As soon as you get a fresh cup of coffee, the boss will ask you to do something that will last until the coffee is cold.

OTTO'S LAW:

You are always doing something marginal when the boss drops by your desk.

BENCHLEY'S LAW:

Anyone can do any amount of work, provided it isn't the work he is supposed to be doing.

CLYDE'S LAW:

If you have something to do, and put it off long enough, chances are that someone else will do it for you.

CHAPMAN'S LAW:

If you can't get your work done in the first 24 hours, work nights.

HARRY'S RULE:

When you don't know what to do, walk fast and look worried.

THE CORRIDOR COROLLARY:

You can go anywhere you want if you look serious and carry a clipboard.

THE FIRST LAW OF THE BUSINESS LETTER:

Never ask two questions in a business letter. The reply will discuss the one you are least interested in, and say nothing about the other.

MATSUI'S LAW OF BUSINESS CALLS:

The most persistent callers have the least important business.

THE PETER-OUT PRINCIPLE:

After any salary raise, you will have less money at the end of the month than you did before.

SOARES'S LAW OF WORKPLACE CLIMATOLOGY:

Repair of the heating system signals the onset of warmer weather.

SHADOW'S LAW:

An unprecedented streak of good weather will be interrupted by rain on your day off.

THOMPSON'S RULE OF WAREHOUSING:

To ensure immediate need of a carton from the shelf, put something very large and heavy in front of it.

SCOTT'S LAW OF COPIERS:

The legibility of a copy is inversely proportional to its importance.

DARWIN'S LAW:

Happiness is not good for work.

THE VACATIONER'S AXIOM:

You always get sick on the second day of your vacation and always recover the day before you return to work.

THE END-TASK RULE:

Everything can be filed under miscellaneous.

HARRINGTON'S LAW:

A clean desk is a sign of a cluttered desk drawer.

Accountsmanship & Legal Murphology

BALZAC'S AXIOM:
Behind every great fortune, there is a crime.

THURBER'S LAW:
There is no safety in numbers, or in anything else.

WINGFIELD'S AXIOM:
Accuracy is the sum total of your compensating mistakes.

CHARLES OSGOOD'S AXIOM:
Nobody thinks they make too much money.

L'ENGLE'S LAW OF ACCOUNTING:
Nobody ever went out of business paying too many taxes because of earning too much money.

RUANE'S LAW OF MONETARY WINDFALLS:
Pennies from heaven are soon followed by a tax collector from hell.

THE FAUVRE PRINCIPLE:
Money earned in your own business will be lost in someone else's business.

MARTIN'S MONEY MAXIM:
It takes a lot of borrowing to live within your income.

CADE'S LAW OF BUDGETING:

The larger the budget, the less effectively the funds are allocated.

SPINOLA'S BUDGET PRINCIPLE:

A budget is just a method of worrying before you spend money, as well as afterward.

GLYNN'S LAW:

The amount of aggravation inherent in a business transaction is inversely proportional to the profit.

SPRUANCE'S LUNCHEON LAW:

The person who suggests splitting the bill evenly is always the person who ordered the most expensive meal.

LAWS OF BANK MERGERS:

1. What's good for your bank is not good for you.
2. Your local branch will be the first one closed.

LAW OF CHECKS AND BALANCES:

In matters of dispute, the bank's balance is always smaller than yours.

THE CALLAWAY'S LAMENT:

Nothing in the known universe travels faster than a bad check.

FIRTH'S THEOREM:

Five is a sufficiently close approximation to infinity.

WINCORN'S LAW:

There are three kinds of people: Those who can count and those who can't.

GUALTIERI'S LAW OF INERTIA:
Where there's a will, there's a won't.

GIBB'S LAW:
Infinity is one lawyer waiting for another.

THE LAWYER'S MAXIM:
Where there's a will, there's a lawsuit.

GREEN'S RULE:
What the large print giveth, the small print taketh away.

ROONEY'S RULE:
Nothing in fine print is ever good news.

MISHLOVE'S LAW:
Never trust a lawyer who says he just slapped something together.

LAWS OF CONTRACT NEGOTIATIONS:

1. Each unacceptable offer has an equal and opposite unreasonable demand.
2. Any concession won is offset by a concession granted.

FIRST LAW OF NEGOTIATION:

A negotiation shall be considered successful if all parties walk away feeling screwed.

JUDGE FANIN'S LAW:

Liability follows damages.

THE AWFUL TRUTH:

Estate planning is not intended to protect your heirs if you die. It is intended to protect your heirs when you die.

MENDELSON'S LAWS:

1. No case settles before it is fully billed.
2. There is no such thing as "our" attorney.

ANDREW YOUNG'S RULE:

Nothing is illegal if a hundred businessmen decide to do it.

MCCANDLISH'S LAW OF UNJUST BUREAUCRACY:

Any system of justice in which ignorance of the law is no excuse, but in which there are too many laws for any one person to know and remember, is by definition unjust.

HENDERSON'S LAW:

The less you say, the less you have to retract.

SPRECHT'S RULE OF LAW:
Under any conditions, anywhere, whatever you are doing, there is some ordinance under which you can be booked.

JUAREZ'S THIRD LAW:
A plea for justice is often a claim for injustice in one's own favor.

BILLING'S LAW:
Silence is one of the hardest things to refute.

BERGEN'S LAW:
There's nothing worse than a stupid law.

Marketplace Murphology

HELEN'S LAW OF BARGAIN SHOPPING:
If you don't buy it when you first see it, it won't be there when you come back.

EVE'S DISCOVERY:
At a bargain sale, the dress you like is the only one not on sale.
Adam's Corollary: It's easy to tell when you've got a bargain—it doesn't fit.

DONNA'S FEMINIST DISCOVERY:
If an article is "specially designed for women," it is the same as a man's model but twice as expensive.

KROUSCUP'S LAW OF SUPPLY:
If you don't need it and don't want it, there is always plenty of it.

SUSSMAN'S ARTWORK PRINCIPLE:
The cost for the framing exceeds the cost of the art.
Corollary: People who bargain over the price of the art will not bargain over the price charged by the framer.

REINHARDT'S GUIDE TO ART:
Sculpture is what you bump into when you back up to look at a painting.

CZLIKNSKY'S LAW OF RETAIL:

If you want to browse, you will be inundated by clerks; if you want to buy, no clerk can be found.

BOOTH'S GROCERY STORE PRINCIPLE:

Regardless of the product you are looking for, someone else's shopping cart will be in front of it.

WALKER'S LAW:

Urgency varies inversely with value.

GERHARDT'S LAW:

If you find something you like, buy a lifetime supply. They are going to stop making it.

PAULSEN'S RULE:

Enter a contest and be on the sponsor's sucker list for life.

THE GLUSKIN-FAGAN RULES:

1. Takeovers are always announced one day after you sell the stock of the target company.
2. Time-tested investment strategies stop working as soon as you put your money into them.
3. The next bull market will begin on the day you swear never to touch another stock as long as you live.
4. The only hot stock market tips that work are those you have ignored.

GINSBURG'S DOW JONES PRINCIPLE:

Major one-day losses are always larger than major one-day gains.

ROBBIN'S RULES OF MARKETING:

1. Your share of the market is lower than you think.
2. The combined market position goals of all competitors always totals at least 150 percent.
3. The existence of a market does not insure the existence of a customer.
4. Beware of alleged needs that have no real market.
5. Low price and long shipment will win over high price and short shipment.
6. If the customer buys lunch, you've lost the order.

MURRAY'S LAW:

Don't believe everything you hear or anything you say.

FREDERICKS'S LAWS OF MARKETING:

1. Never listen to your own hype.

2. Never get downwind from your marketing.

THIRD RULE FOR RETAILERS:

The customer is almost right.

THE LAW OF OVERSELL:

When putting cheese in a mousetrap, always leave room for the mouse.

SAY'S LAW:

Supply creates its own demand.

PANGER'S ADVERTISING PRINCIPLE:

Nobody buys a half-truth, but some will swallow a whole lie.

FIRST RULE OF FOREIGN SALES:

Any foreign payments will be at the worst possible exchange rate.

THE BANKING PRINCIPLE:

When you get to the front of the line, the teller will close.

Corollary: The "Use Next Window" sign will point to a window that is also closed.

ETORRE'S OBSERVATION:

The other line moves faster.

THE LINEAR ACCELERATOR PRINCIPLE:

The shorter the line, the slower it moves.

LANGER'S LAW:

If the line moves quickly, you're in the wrong line.

Travel, Roadsmanship & Sportsmanship

THE ECLIPSE PRINCIPLE:
The longer you travel to view an eclipse, the greater the chance of cloud cover.

THE RENT-A-CAR LAW:
In any airport served by several car rental agencies, the other service shuttles will arrive before yours.

JEFF'S LAW OF RENTAL CARS:
When buying gas for a rental car, nine times out of ten you will pull up to the wrong side of the gas pump.

LORENZ'S LAW OF MECHANICAL REPAIR:
After your hands become coated with grease, your nose will begin to itch.

FIRMAGE'S RULE OF AUTO REPAIR:
That which is attached with only two bolts is directly behind something attached with eight.

CUSAK'S OBSERVATION:
The driver's-side windshield wiper always wears out first.
Corollary: The worst smear is at eye level.

RANDALL'S LAW OF AUTOMOTIVES:
The flat doesn't occur until the day after the tire sale.

ROB'S LAMENT:
As soon as you become familiar with all the shortcuts and secret parking places in town, you will be transferred to a different town.

HYMAN'S HIGHWAY HYPOTHESIS:
The shortest distance between two points is usually under construction.

BENEDICT'S LAW OF CARPOOLING:
As soon as you switch to the carpool lane, the other lanes of traffic speed up.

GRELB'S FRIGHTENING THOUGHT:
Eighty percent of all people consider themselves to be above average drivers.

WEXFORD'S LAW:
In a two-car family, the wife always has the smaller car.
Berris's Exception: If the husband wants a giant off-road vehicle, the wife will have to drive it during the week.

RENNIE'S LAW OF PUBLIC TRANSIT:
If you start walking, the bus will come when you are precisely halfway between stops.

DALE'S PARKING POSTULATE:
If only two cars are left in a parking lot, one will be blocking the other.

JAROSLOVSKY'S LAW:

The distance you have to park from your apartment increases in proportion to the weight of packages you are carrying.

HIGHWAY TRAVELER'S RULE OF BILLBOARDS:

The quality of the food is inversely proportional to the distance of the first roadside advertisement.

THE MOTEL MAXIM:

The person who will leave the earliest has parked his car in front of your window.

THE MCGWIRE PRINCIPLE:

The biggest plays occur when you're out buying beer.

RITA'S RULE:

The one time you don't put money in the meter will coincide with the one daily visit of the meter maid.

GILBERT'S LAW OF SPORTS:

Wherever you park, your seats will be on the other side of the stadium.

ANTON'S LAW OF STADIUMS AND ARENAS:

When they keep the price of tickets down, the cost of parking goes up.

THE STADIUM SERVICE PRINCIPLE:

The quality of food and service varies inversely with the number of alternative sources available.

Corollary: When there is only one concessionaire, the price will be exhorbitant.

EMILY'S RULE OF SPORTING EVENTS (THE SUPER BOWL PRINCIPLE):

The more highly anticipated the sporting event, the less exciting it will be.

DOC MARTIN'S LAWS OF FOOTBALL:

1. Your best play of the day will be nullified by a minor penalty.

2. Your opponents will make first downs by inches; you will come up short by inches.

3. Your most valuable player will be the first to be injured.

GRIGGS'S LAW OF INDIVIDUAL PERFORMANCE:

The day you set the record, your team will lose the game.

LAS VEGAS LAW:

The probability of winning is inversely proportional to the amount of the wager.

IRV'S LAW OF GOLF:
Any swing improvement will only last three holes.

TAYLOR'S PUTTING PRINCIPLE:
Any putt is straight if you hit it hard enough.

BENTON'S LAW OF GOLF:
Demo clubs only work until you buy them.

FELT'S LAW OF GOLF:
The first time you three-putt will be on the first green you hit in regulation.

ANDERSON'S LAW OF GOLF:
The player furthest from tee after the first shot will be furthest from the hole after the second shot.

SID'S LAW:
You can't win them all if you don't win the first one.

FIRST LAW OF SPELUNKING:
Never try to crawl through a hole smaller than your head.

G. DAVID'S LAW:
It doesn't matter if you win or lose . . . until you lose.

PSycHO-MurpHOLOgy oF Everyday LiFe

HUGO'S HOMILY:
Eat one live toad the first thing in the morning and nothing worse will happen to you the rest of the day.

KRANSKE'S LAW:
Beware of a day during which you don't have something to complain about.

W. C. FIELDS'S MAXIM:
Start every day off with a smile and get it over with.

R. C. GALLAGHER'S LAW:
Change is inevitable—except from a vending machine.

BUTNER'S LAW:
He who laughs last, thinks slowest.

CARSON'S LAWS OF COMEDY:
1. If they buy the premise, they'll buy the bit.
2. Don't do more than three jokes on the same premise.

LAW OF TALENT SHOWS:
The best performer in your category will go on just before you do.

YELLIN'S LAW:

The probability of winning the lottery is slightly greater if you buy a ticket.

YELLIN'S THEATRE LAW:

The tallest person in the audience will sit down in front of you only after it is too late for you to find another seat.

CHEKHOV'S LAW:
If there is a gun hanging on the wall in the first act, it must fire in the last.

PINGATORE'S POSTAL PRINCIPLE:
People usually get what's coming to them . . . unless it's been mailed.

AVERY'S OBSERVATION:
It does not matter if you fall down as long as you pick up something from the floor while you get up.

BERKSHIRE'S LAW OF HOUSEHOLD BUDGETING:
Just after you've made both ends meet, someone moves the ends.

STETTNER'S FOOD LAW:
The more you enjoy something, the worse it is for you.

SUSANNA'S LAW:
Every recipe includes one ingredient that you do not have in your kitchen.
Corollary: If the ingredient is essential, your grocer will be out of stock.

TEMPLE'S LAW OF THE KITCHEN:
Anything cooked in an oven will be either over-cooked or undercooked.
Corollary: Anything cooked in a microwave oven will be overcooked and undercooked at the same time.

PULLIAM'S POSTULATE:
Never step in anything soft.

CRANSTON'S DELI LAW:
The larger the menu, the sooner the waitress comes to ask for your order.

LANGFIELD'S LAW OF GASTRONOMY:
The discovery of a new dish is more beneficial to humanity than the discovery of a new star.

ISAAC'S STRANGE RULE OF STALENESS:
Any food that starts out hard will soften when stale. Any food that starts out soft will harden when stale.

BARBARA'S LAW:
Never say "wow" with food in your mouth.

GROWN CHILD'S LAMENT:
Mother said there would be days like this, but she never said there would be so many.

BOMBECK'S LAW OF HEREDITY:
Insanity is hereditary; you get it from your kids.

MOM'S LAW:
A show-off is any child who is more talented than yours.

THE THREE WAYS TO GET SOMETHING DONE:
1. Do it yourself.
2. Hire someone to do it for you.
3. Forbid your kids to do it.

F. P. JONES'S OBSERVATION:
Children are unpredictable. You never know what inconsistency they're going to catch you in next.

BARNHILL'S SPARE BUTTON PRINCIPLE:
Shirts that come with extra buttons never lose buttons.

CLIFF'S LAW:
Never stand between a dog and a hydrant.

CORY'S LAW OF PARENTING:
Children become noisy as soon as you get on the telephone.

Zellie's Corollary: The worse the phone connection, the louder the kids get.

FANT'S LAW:
When attempting to open a locked door with only one hand free, the key will be in the opposite pocket.

LOVKA'S HOUSEHOLD MAXIM:

If you think you left it on and return to check it, it will be off; if you think you might have left it on and don't return to check it, it will be on.

MRS. FERGUS'S OBSERVATION:

The lost sock reappears only after its match has been discarded.

THE LEATHER/WEATHER RULE:

The chance of a sudden cloudburst is in direct proportion to the amount of suede you are wearing.

TIBBETTS'S LAW OF OPPORTUNITY:

The only time the world beats a path to your door is when you are in the bathroom.

SAVAGE'S LAW:

The leak in the roof is never in the same location as the drip.

CARLYLE'S MYSTERY KEY THEORY:

On a keyring with multiple keys, there will always be one key that does not open anything.

THE REJA-JANSEN LAW:

On the first pull of the cord, the drapes will move the wrong way.

ANGELA'S AXIOM:

The last sheet of gift wrap will be six inches smaller than the last gift to wrap.

JEAN'S LAW:

The lightest-colored fabric attracts the darkest-colored stain.

Laws For the Millennium
(and For those Who Never thought they'd get there)

HUXLEY ON PROGRESS:
Technological progress has merely provided us with more efficient means for going backwards.

OGDEN NASH'S LAW:
Progress may have been all right once, but it went on too long.
M. L. 2000 Corollary: To those who insist that progress is good, mention voice mail.

ELLIS'S LAW:
Progress is the exchange of one nuisance for another.

ENGLER'S RULE OF INNOVATION:
Innovation requires bypassing—not building upon—existing expertise.

REISNER'S RULE OF CONCEPTUAL INERTIA:
If you think big enough, you'll never have to do it.

LINTON'S LAW:
Growth is directly proportional to promises made; profit is inversely proportional to promises kept.

KURTIN'S LAW OF SURVIVAL:
It's not who is right, it's who is left.

GERHARD'S OBSERVATION:
We're making progress. Things are getting worse at a slower rate.

JERRY'S LAW:
Just because everything is different doesn't mean anything has changed.

COOPER'S LAW:
Nothing will be attempted if all possible objections must first be overcome.

BREZNIKAR'S INTEREST PRINCIPLE:
Almost everything is more popular than it used to be.

FRIED'S LAW:
Ideas endure and prosper in inverse proportion to their soundness and validity.

WHITEHEAD'S LEMMA:
Civilization advances by extending the number of important operations that we can perform without thinking about them.

SHAW'S OBSERVATION:
The reasonable man adapts himself to the world; the unreasonable one persists in trying to adapt the world to himself. Therefore all progress depends on the unreasonable man.

ZIGGY'S LAW:
Do a little more each day than everyone expects and soon everyone will expect more.

ELLIOTT'S AXIOM:
All children are future ex-idealists.

PIERSON'S LAW:
   If you're coasting, you're going downhill.

HARRISON'S POSTULATE:
For every action, there is an equal and opposite criticism.

KELLY'S OBSERVATION:
Living in the past has one thing in its favor—it's cheaper.

CAPP'S LAW:
The closest you can get to your youth is to start repeating your follies.

DUMPER'S PRINCIPLE OF NEOTONY:
An adult is a deteriorated child.

ANDERSON'S AXIOM:
You can only be young once, but you can be immature forever.

TALLULAH BANKHEAD'S OBSERVATION:
If I had to live my life again, I'd make the same mistakes, only sooner.

ERTZ'S OBSERVATION:
Millions long for immortality who don't know what to do on a rainy Sunday afternoon.

GRIMES'S LAW:
Nostalgia is the realization that things weren't as unbearable as they seemed at the time.

KUBIN'S MAXIM:
How feeble are Man's efforts against the unyielding forces of Nature—until the struggle is recounted for the grandchildren.

DUEZABOU'S OBSERVATION:

If you abstain from drinking, smoking and carousing, you may not live longer—but it will feel longer.

RUSSELL'S RULE:

Don't worry about avoiding temptation—as you grow older, it starts avoiding you.

SHAW'S MAXIM:

Virtue is insufficient temptation.

PETERSON'S PRINCIPLE:

Traditions are solutions for which we have forgotten the problems.

BAKER'S BY-LAW:

When you are over the hill, you pick up speed.

LINUS'S LAW:

There is no heavier burden than a great potential.

Transcendental Murphology

JAMES'S PRINCIPLE:
There is no greater lie than a truth misunderstood.

HORACE'S WARNING:
Beware of the superficially profound.

IRISHMAN'S LEMMA:
Faith is believin' what you know ain't so.

HOLMES'S HOMILY:
It is well to remember that the entire universe, with one trifling exception, is composed of others.

WILDE ON MAN AND GOD:
God in creating man somewhat overestimated his ability.

HEISENBERG'S LAW:
There are things that are so serious that you can only joke about them.

RUSSELL'S OBSERVATION:
The point of philosophy is to start with something so simple as to seem not worth stating, and to end with something so paradoxical that no one will believe it.

TOYNBEE'S RULE:
In matters of religion, it is very easy to deceive mankind and very difficult to undeceive them.

FATHER FITZGERALD'S RULE:
Behave as if you were watched.

MILLAY'S MAXIM:
It is not true that life is one damn thing after another—it's one damn thing over and over.

DEFALQUE'S OBSERVATION:
A path without obstacles usually leads nowhere.

MUMFORD'S MAXIM:
Traditionalists are pessimists about the future and optimists about the past.

ROSTAND'S COMMENT:
My pessimism extends to the point of even suspecting the sincerity of other pessimists.

AQUINAS'S WARNING:
Beware the man of one book.

THE OLD PORTER'S OBSERVATION:
There's very few what comes up to the average.

BERRA'S ADVICE:
When you come to a fork in the road, take it.

FRIEDMAN'S OBSERVATION:
Human beings are distinguished from other animals more by their ability to rationalize than their ability to reason.

THE VOICE-MAIL PRINCIPLE:
Those whom the gods wish to destroy, they first put on hold.

R. A. WILSON'S RULE:
Reality is whatever you can get away with.

P. K. DICK'S RULE:
Reality is what refuses to go away when you stop believing in it.

DICK'S LEMMA:
Just because you're paranoid doesn't mean they're not out to get you.

GUTIERREZ'S LAW:
The only true freedom is freedom from choice.

EINSTEIN ON LIFE:
1. Reality is merely an illusion, albeit a very persistent one.
2. Imagination is more important than knowledge.
3. The only real valuable thing is intuition.
4. Everything should be made as simple as possible, but not simpler.
5. Common sense is the collection of prejudices acquired by age eighteen.
6. Gravitation is not responsible for people falling in love.

LARSON'S LAW:
A lot of people mistake a short memory for a clear conscience.

SANTAYANA'S FIRST LAW:
Sanity is madness put to good use.

WILDE'S THEORY:
Only the shallow know themselves.

SAUGET'S LAW:
Sit at the feet of the master long enough and they start to smell.

ROOSEVELT'S RULE:
When you get to the end of your rope, tie a knot and hang on.

CLARKE'S LAW OF EVOLUTION:
It has yet to be proven that intelligence has any survival value.

SYRUS'S AXIOM:
Not every question deserves an answer.

VOLTAIRE'S MAXIM:
A witty saying proves nothing.

Heard a good Law lately? If you have, or you've come up with one yourself and you'd like to see it immortalized in print, why not send it to us for inclusion in a future *Murphy's Law* book or calendar? If the Law you send is from another source, please try to tell us exactly where it came from. Send your Laws to:

Murphy's Law
c/o 2560 9th Street, Suite 123
Berkeley, CA 94710

or email it to:
MurphysLaw2000@hotmail.com